A Gift WORTH KEEPING

Written by DORI SCHUBRING

Illustrated by ZYBRENA PORTER

WestBow Press books may be ordered through booksellers or by contacting:

WestBow Press
A Division of Thomas Nelson & Zondervan
1663 Liberty Drive
Bloomington, IN 47403
www.westbowpress.com
844-714-3454

Interior Image Credit: Zybrena Porter

Scripture quotations marked * or NLT are taken from the Holy Bible, New Living Translation, Copyright © 1996, 2004, 2015 by Tyndale House Foundation. Used by permission of Tyndale House Publishers, Inc., Carol Stream, Illinois 60188. All rights reserved.

Scripture quotations marked ** or NIV are taken from The Holy Bible, New International Version®, NIV® Copyright © 1973, 1978, 1984, 2011 by Biblica, Inc.® Used by permission. All rights reserved worldwide.

ISBN: 978-1-6642-4492-4 (sc)
ISBN: 978-1-6642-4494-8 (hc)
ISBN: 978-1-6642-4493-1 (e)

Library of Congress Control Number: 2021918905

Print information available on the last page.

WestBow Press rev. date: 10/21/2021

WESTBOW
PRESS®
A DIVISION OF THOMAS NELSON
& ZONDERVAN

Acknowledgments

We thank God for giving Dori this story idea more than fourteen years ago and for putting Zybrena in her path to do the amazing illustrations!

Thanks to our incredible husbands, Paul and C.J., for their unfailing support and encouragement.

Thank you to each of our children for showing us that you truly are gifts from God.

Thanks to Justin, Gabe, Joshua, Niall, Ayla, and Aryan for allowing us to use their baby photos.

Thanks to Nancy for introducing us!

Thanks to all who are actively involved in promoting and celebrating the gift of life.

Introduction

Life is about journeys. Moving from one point in time to another. This is a story about my journey as a fetus, beginning inside my mother's womb and ending on the day of my birth. The story is based on biblical passages that tell us about God's plan for humanity.

I believe that God makes Himself known to every child as they are developing and growing inside their mother's womb. I can picture Him talking to, comforting, nurturing, teaching, and keeping every precious little fetus company until his or her grand entrance into this world. I believe that God fills up the tiny child's spirit with His presence so that every child is born with a connection to their Heavenly Father and Creator.

However you feel about the child in the womb—be it excited, thankful, scared, confused, or alone—this story may help you, as a mother, discover that the life growing inside you was not placed there by accident. That child is a gift. A gift worth keeping. And I dedicate this book to every single one.

"Children are a gift from the LORD; they are a reward from Him"

(Psalm 127:3*).

It's hard to remember before I was born—so safe, warm, and perfect. I was already growing from a single cell, a miracle being created by God.

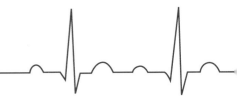

"But even before I was born, God chose me and called me by his marvelous grace" (Galatians 1:15*).

The embryo's first heartbeat begins as early as 21 days after conception. Before a woman knows she is pregnant, this life inside her is alive and growing.[1]

He came to me in the darkness. My Father, Creator, Teacher, Savior, and Friend. He talked to me, and He kept me company. I was never alone and never afraid.

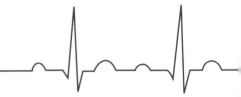

"...And be sure of this: I am with you always, even to the end of the age" (Matthew 28:20*).

By 4 weeks, your baby is about 1/8 inch long, which is the length of a grain of rice. Her brain and major organs are already developing![2]

He told me to kick because it would make my legs strong. And it did.

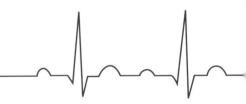

"God arms me with strength, and he makes my way perfect" (Psalm 18:32*).

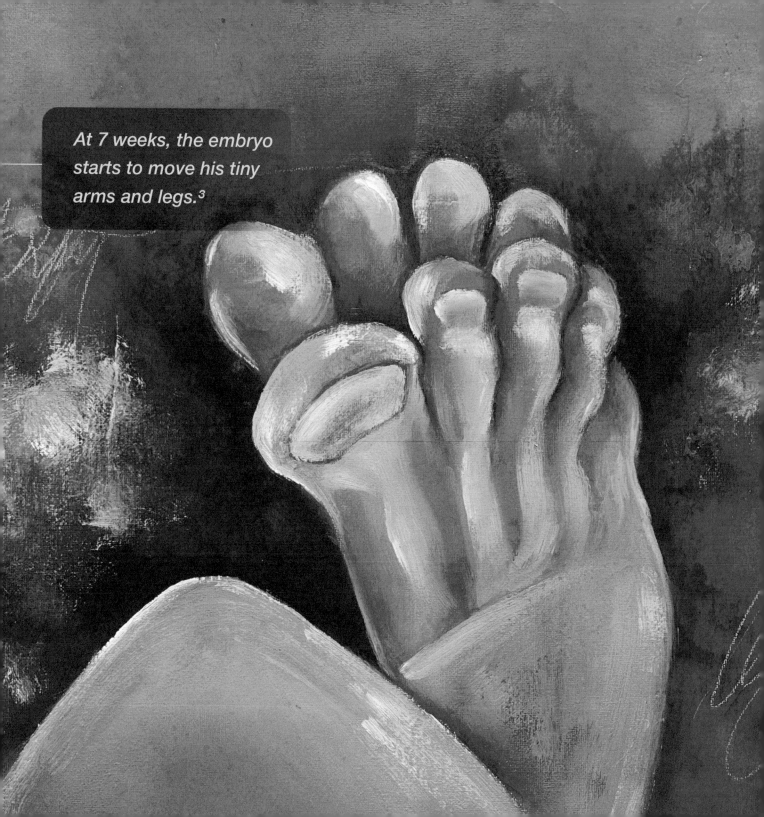

At 7 weeks, the embryo starts to move his tiny arms and legs.[3]

He told me to roll and turn and flip around so I could feel

what it was like to move my growing body. And I did.

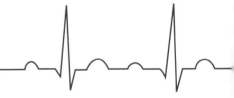

"For you created my inmost being; you knit me together
in my mother's womb" (Psalm 139:13**).

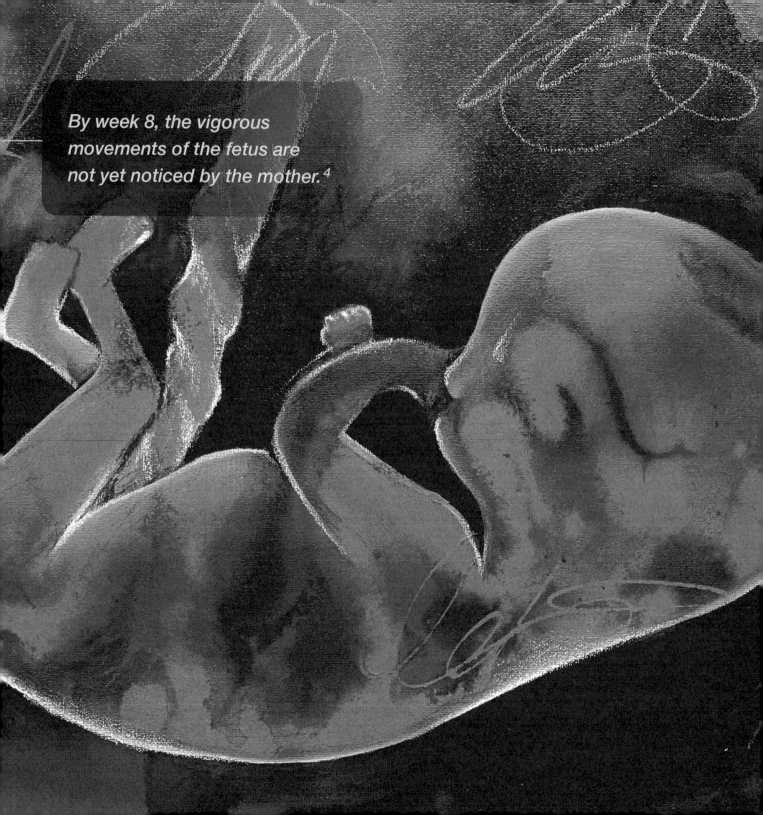

God told me that I am unique *and* that

no one will be exactly like me.

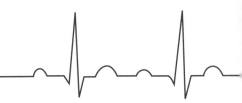

"For we are God's handiwork, created in Christ Jesus to do good works, which God prepared in advance for us to do" (Ephesians 2:10**).

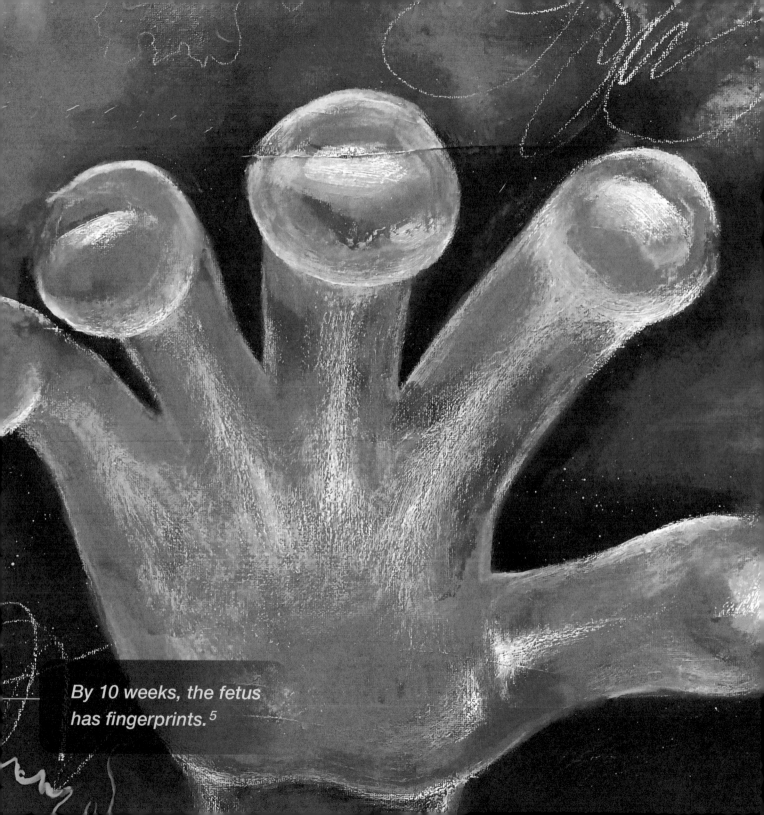

By 10 weeks, the fetus has fingerprints. [5]

He told me I could suck my thumb when I felt fear, stress,

or uncertainty because it would soothe me. And it did.

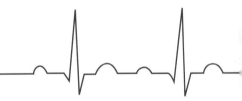

"This is what the LORD says—he who made you,
who formed you in the womb, and who will help
you: Do not be afraid..." (Isaiah 44:2**).

At 9 to 12 weeks, a fetus starts to suck her thumb. [6]

He told me to listen with my ears so I could recognize my mom's voice after I was born. He said her familiar voice would comfort me. And it did.

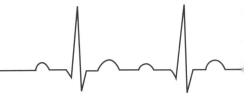

"...Before I was born the LORD called me; from my mother's womb he has spoken my name" (Isaiah 49:1**).

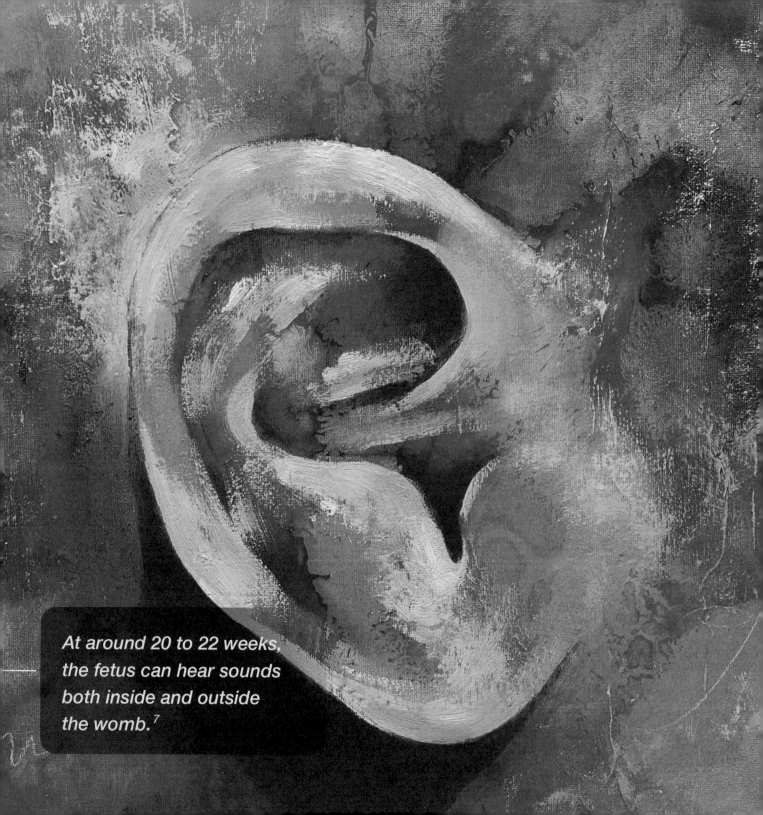

At around 20 to 22 weeks, the fetus can hear sounds both inside and outside the womb.[7]

He told me to open my eyes so that I could see

my family after I was born. And I did.

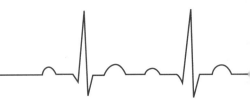

"But it was your own eyes that saw all these great
things the LORD has done" (Deuteronomy 11:7**).

At around 24 weeks, the fetus can open and close his eyes.[8]

God told me that I would serve a very important purpose in my mother's life. He said that I would help her grasp how much He loves her. God told me that I am a special gift *and* that He has great plans for me.

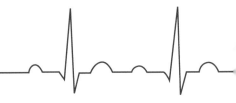

"'For I know the plans I have for you,' declares the Lord, 'plans to prosper you and not to harm you, plans to give you hope and a future'" (Jeremiah 29:11**).

A mother may feel her baby's first movements anytime between 13 and 25 weeks. [9]

God told me that it will be different out there. It will seem strange at first, and it will be difficult. I will have many challenges along the way. But then God told me to remember this: "You are mine. I created you. I will always love you."

"And I am convinced that nothing can ever separate us from God's love..." (Romans 8:38*).

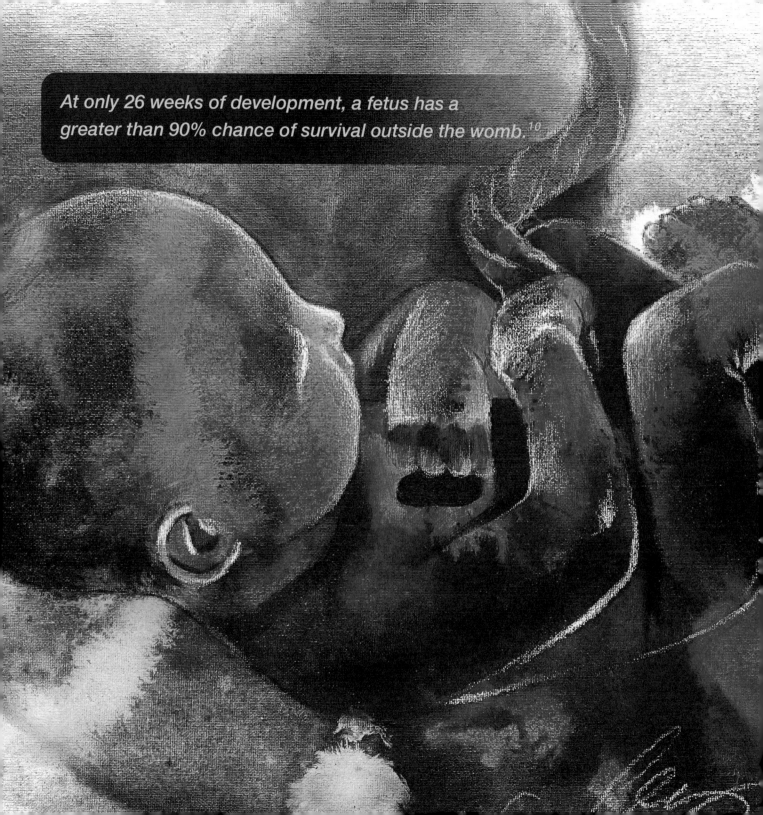

At only 26 weeks of development, a fetus has a greater than 90% chance of survival outside the womb.[10]

He even told me when to be born because this was the special delivery day God had planned just for me—the day I would see the outside world and meet my family. And I did.

"Yet you brought me out of the womb; you made me trust in you, even at my mother's breast. From birth I was cast on you; from my mother's womb You have been my God" (Psalm 22:9-10**).

A baby is considered full term when born between 39 and 40 weeks.[11]

Every child is a gift that is unique, beautiful, wonderful, and special. May God bless every child who is not yet conceived or not yet born. You're a gift worth keeping.

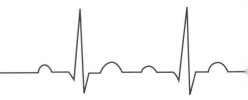

"Let this be written for a future generation, that a people not yet created may praise the LORD" (Psalm 102:18**).

Who Am I?

God made me.
Genesis 1:27 • Psalm 139:13 • Isaiah 44:24

God planned and purposed me.
Jeremiah 29:11 • Psalm 102:18 • Jeremiah 1:5

God put His spirit in me.
Isaiah 59:21 • Romans 8:16

God knows everything about me.
Matthew 10:30

God loves me.
John 3:16 • 1 John 3:1 • 1 John 4:16

God says I'm a gift!
Psalm 127:3 • James 1:17

References

Ages given are referenced as fetal ages, which are based on the dates of conception or fertilization. It is noted that there are many references on fetal development and many of the milestones are acquired in a range of weeks as opposed to a single time frame.

1   Heritage House '76, Inc. *Milestones of Early Life.* Snowflake, AZ: Heritage House '76, Inc. 2018. www.hh76.com. "Baby's Heartbeat." Just the Facts. (n.d.). https://www.justthefacts.org/get-the-facts/babys-heartbeat/.

2   Heritage House '76, Inc. *Milestones of Early Life.* Snowflake, AZ: Heritage House '76, Inc. 2018. www.hh76.com.

3   Heritage House '76, Inc. *Milestones of Early Life.* Snowflake, AZ: Heritage House '76, Inc. 2018. www.hh76.com.

4   Heritage House '76, Inc. *Milestones of Early Life.* Snowflake, AZ: Heritage House '76, Inc. 2018. www.hh76.com. The Endowment for Human Development. (n.d.). *Spontaneous Movement Movie #046.* ehd.org. https://www.ehd.org/movies/46/Spontaneous-Movement.

5   Heritage House '76, Inc. *Milestones of Early Life.* Snowflake, AZ: Heritage House '76, Inc. 2018. www.hh76.com. The Endowment for Human Development. (n.d.). *Nails and Fingerprints Movie #061.* ehd.org. https://www.ehd.org/movies/61/Nails-and-Fingerprints.

6   The Endowment for Human Development (n.d.). *Prenatal Form and Function-The Making of an Earth Suit Unit 9: 8-9weeks.*ehd.org. https://www.ehd.org/dev_article_unit9.php.

7   *Prenatal Summary.* ehd.org. (n.d.). https://www.ehd.org/prenatal-summary.php.

8   *Prenatal Summary.* ehd.org. (n.d.). https://www.ehd.org/prenatal-summary.php.

9   American Pregnancy Association (n.d.). *First Fetal Movement: Quickening.* americanpregnancy.org. https://americanpregnancy.org/healthy-pregnancy/pregnancyhealth-wellness/first-fetal-movement/.

10 Bird, C. (June 21, 2021). *Micro Preemie Survival Rates and Health Concerns.* verywellfamily.com. https://www.verywellfamily.com/what-is-a-micro-preemie2748625.

11 National Child & Maternal Health Education Program (n.d.). *Know Your Terms.* Eunice Kennedy Shriver National Institute of Child Health and Human Development. https://www.nichd.nih.gov/ncmhep/initiatives/know-your-terms/moms.

Printed in the United States
by Baker & Taylor Publisher Services